"But the Pension Fund Was Just Sitting There"

Doonesbury books by G.B. Trudeau

Still a Few Bugs in the System
The President Is a Lot Smarter Than You Think
But This War Had Such Promise
Call Me When You Find America
Guilty, Guilty, Guilty!
"What Do We Have for the Witnesses, Johnnie?"
Dare To Be Great, Ms. Caucus
Wouldn't a Gremlin Have Been More Sensible?
"Speaking of Inalienable Rights, Amy..."
You're Never Too Old for Nuts and Berries
An Especially Tricky People
As the Kid Goes for Broke
Stalking the Perfect Tan
"Any Grooming Hints for Your Fans, Rollie?"
"But the Pension Fund Was Just Sitting There"

In Large Format

The Doonesbury Chronicles
Doonesbury's Greatest Hits

a Doonesbury classic by

G B Trudeau.

"But the Pension Fund Was Just Sitting There"

An Owl Book Holt, Rinehart and Winston / New York

Published by Holt, Rinehart and Winston,
383 Madison Avenue,
New York, New York 10017.

Published simultaneously in Canada
by Holt, Rinehart and Winston
of Canada, Limited.

Library of Congress Catalog Card Number: 74-14165

ISBN: 0-03-049176-2

Printed in the United States of America

The cartoons in this book have appeared in newspapers
in the United States and abroad under the auspices of
Universal Press Syndicate.

6 8 10 9 7 5

ISBN 0-03-049176-2

..AND ART BUCHWALD'S NOT AVAILABLE EITHER, WHICH MEANS WE'VE GOT ONLY **ONE** WEEK LEFT TO FIND SOMEONE TO GIVE THIS YEAR'S JOURNALISM LECTURE!

ABE, I'VE GOT A SUGGESTION! HOW ABOUT FORMER AMBASSADOR DUKE, THE EX-GONZO STRINGER FOR "ROLLING STONE"?

HIS IS A UNIQUE PERSPECTIVE ON THE DARK UNDERSIDE OF OUTLAW JOURNALISM. AND HIS IMMENSE POPULARITY AMONG US KIDS WOULD LEND A CACHET TO THE LECTURE!

ACCORDING TO WHOM?

ZONKER. I'VE NEVER HEARD OF HIM MYSELF.

TRUST ME, GUYS. HE'D BE PERFECT! REALLY!

GB Trudeau

MR. DUKE, I'M THINKING OF BECOMING A REPORTER. WHAT ADVICE WOULD YOU GIVE SOMEONE WHO IS JUST START-ING OUT?

LOOK, JUNIOR, JOURNALISM IS A JUNGLE! NEVER FORGET THAT! IN JOURNALISM, THERE ARE NO WINNERS, JUST SURVIVORS! WE ARE TALKING SNAKE PIT CITY, SLIM!

SO DIG IT! I BEEN THERE! IF YOU FALTER FOR A SECOND, YOUR COLLEAGUES WILL WASTE YOU, WILL SAVAGE YOUR REP, YOUR NAME, YOUR.. YOUR..

WHAT WAS THE QUESTION AGAIN?

UM.. HOW DO YOU LIKE OUR CAMPUS?

GBTrudeau

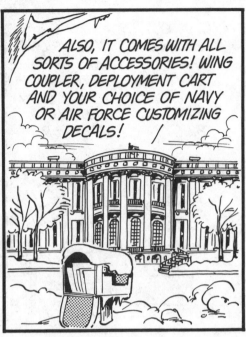

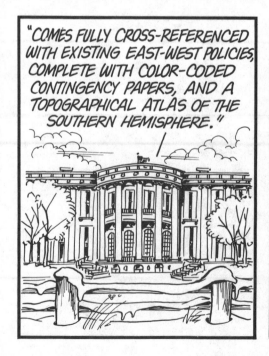

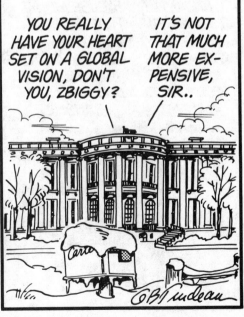

IN OTHER NEWS, THE SHAH OF IRAN HAS DISPATCHED HIS WIFE, THE SHAHBANOU FARAH, ON YET ANOTHER PUBLIC RELATIONS TOUR OF THE UNITED STATES.

THE FIRST DINNER IN HER HONOR WILL BE IN NEW YORK CITY, WHERE MAYOR KOCH IS EXPECTED TO EARMARK $1 MILLION TO PAY FOR POLICE PROTECTION FOR THE EMPRESS..

THE DINNER'S INVITED SPEAKER IS DR. HENRY KISSINGER, BUT KISSINGER'S GEORGETOWN UNIVERSITY STUDENTS ARE SAID TO BE ORGANIZING A FORMAL PROTEST OF HIS PARTICIPATION.

I TAKE IT NONE OF YOU HAS DONE THE READING TODAY..

DON'T TRY TO CHANGE THE SUBJECT, DOC!

GOOD EVENING. THIS IS THE SCENE IN NEW YORK TONIGHT AS HUNDREDS OF DEMONSTRATORS GATHER OUTSIDE A DINNER FOR THE EMPRESS OF IRAN. ROLAND HEDLEY IS THERE.

HARRY, THERE'S BEEN A SLIGHT DELAY IN THE FESTIVITIES TONIGHT AS WE AWAIT THE LATE ARRIVAL OF PRO-SHAH FORCES HERE AT THE NEW YORK HILTON HOTEL.

BAD WEATHER APPARENTLY DELAYED THE BUSES BRINGING THE SHAH'S RECRUITS TO N.Y., SO OUT OF FAIRNESS, PLANNERS HAVE HELD UP THE BANQUET TO ALLOW COUNTERDEMONSTRATORS TIME TO TAKE UP THEIR POSITIONS!

LONG LIVE THE SHAH!

..AND HERE THEY COME NOW! LOOKS LIKE THE EVENING'S UNDER WAY, HARRY!

GBTrudeau

WITH THE SERVING OF A PÂTÉ DE FOIE GRAS AND A LIGHT CHABLIS, THE FRIENDS OF EXXON SOCIETY DINNER HONORING THE SHAHBANOU FARAH IS FINALLY UNDER WAY, HARRY..

DESPITE THE UGLY PROTESTS OUTSIDE, SOME OF OUR BRIGHTEST STARS HAVE TURNED OUT, RANGING FROM VACATIONING NEWSMAN WALTER CRONKITE TO TONIGHT'S BIGGEST SURPRISE, ACTIVIST SHIRLEY MACLAINE!

THE SHAH IS A **MURDERER!** THE SHAH IS A **MUR-DERER!!**

THE SHAH IS.. **AWK!**

WELL, THE SPEECHES HAVE ALREADY BEGUN HERE AT THE HILTON BALLROOM, HARRY..

"THE SHAH IS A MURDERER!"

HARRY, THE SITUATION HERE ON THE BALLROOM FLOOR IS BEGINNING TO HEAT UP, TO SAY THE LEAST.

EVEN AS I SPEAK, ONE TUXEDOED GENTLEMAN SHOUTING "THE SHAH IS A MURDERER" IS BEING WRESTLED TO THE GROUND BY FOUR DECORUM-MINDED IRANIAN SECURITY AGENTS.

SCUFFLE!
SCUFFLE!

PRESUMABLY TO STIFLE HIS OUTBURSTS, A NAPKIN IS NOW BEING STUFFED IN THE MAN'S MOUTH, AN UNNECESSARY MEASURE IN THIS REPORTER'S JUDGMENT, AS A NASTY RABBIT PUNCH HAS ALREADY TAKEN AWAY HIS WIND!

DEMITASSE, SIR?

FOR THE EMPRESS'S REACTION, UP TO YOU AT THE HEAD TABLE, BARBARA!

GBTrudeau

DAN, I THINK THE QUESTION THAT MANY PEOPLE MIGHT HAVE FOR YOU NOW IS, "WHAT WITH ALL THE CUISINARTS, TENNIS LESSONS AND TR-4'S, CAN I REALLY *AFFORD* MELLOW?"

I HEAR YOU, MARK. ONE OF THE MOST COMMON MISCONCEPTIONS ABOUT MELLOW TODAY IS THAT YOU HAVE TO BE UPWARDLY MO-BILE, ECONOMICWISE, BEFORE YOU CAN FLASH ON IT!

WELL, IT JUST ISN'T SO! IN FACT, THE EXTENSIVE RESEARCH I DID DURING MY FELLOWSHIP AT THE CALIFORNIA INSTITUTE FOR THE MELLOW STRONGLY SUGGESTS OTHERWISE!

FELLOWSHIP? YOU WERE A MELLOW FELLOW?

IT'S ALL IN MY CHAPTER, "MELLOW ON A FIXED INCOME."

HOWDY, CAMPERS, THIS IS "PROFILES ON PARADE." I'M "MARVELOUS" MARK SLACKMEYER, AND MY SPECIAL GUEST TODAY IS NONE OTHER THAN.. MY FATHER!

DAD'S A SUCCESSFUL BROKER, AND HE'S HERE ON CAMPUS FOR HIS 35TH REUNION. HE'S HAD A PRETTY DARN INTERESTING LIFE, SO WITHOUT ANY FURTHER ADO, I'LL JUST OPEN THE LINES UP FOR QUESTIONS! CALL US AT 331-9100!

THAT NUMBER AGAIN..

WHAT SEEMS TO BE THE PROBLEM?

LET ME SET IT UP FOR YOU, FREDDY. THE GUY ON THE LEFT IS LEONARD. HE RUNS A WOMEN'S HEALTH SPA IN LOS ANGELES!

OUR JIGGLE INTEREST IS MUFFY, THE PHYSICAL THERAPIST. THE RUNNING GAG IS THAT EVERY TIME LEONARD GOES IN TO CHECK THE SAUNA, THERE'S MUFFY!

WE THINK THAT CHRISSY LANG, THE GIRL WHO PLAYS MUFFY, IS A MAJOR, BUT MAJOR, TALENT! WE THINK SHE COULD MAKE "SPA" THE HOTTEST SHOW ON T.V.!

GREAT STUFF. DOES SHE HAVE ANY LINES?

WELL, NOT AT FIRST. WE WANT TO ESTABLISH HER CHARACTER.

THIS IS ROLAND BURTON HEDLEY, JR.! AT ROCKEFELLER CENTER TONIGHT, TENSIONS ARE MOUNTING AS THE NBC TELEVISION NETWORK AWAITS ITS NEW MESSIAH, FRED P. SILVERMAN.

CAN THE GENIUS BEHIND "THE LOVE BOAT" AND "CAPTAIN CAVEMAN AND THE TEENANGELS" RESTORE THE FORTUNES OF LAST-PLACE NBC? A RECENT DEVELOPMENT SUGGESTS HE MIGHT..

ABC WIDE WORLD OF NEWS HAS LEARNED THAT WHEN FREDDY SILVERMAN ARRIVES AT NBC THIS WEEK, HE WILL PROPOSE A POLICY OF PRIME-TIME *FRONTAL NUDITY!*

ALSO, CHIMPS. BUT WE'LL GET TO THAT LATER. FOR DETAILS ON THE NUDITY, LET'S GO TO CHICAGO..

CHICAGO?

HEEWACK! COMMANDER HARRIS HERE, KIDDIES, WITH ANOTHER EDITION OF "PROFILES ON PARADE"!

AS YOU MAY KNOW, TODAY MARKS THE SILVER ANNIVERSARY OF THE HOUSE ETHICS COMMITTEE'S INVESTIGATION INTO KOREAGATE, AND TO CELEBRATE, WE SENT OUR OWN MARK SLACKMEYER TO THE NATION'S CAPITAL!

HE'S STANDING BY RIGHT NOW WITH CONGRESS-LADY LACEY DAVENPORT, A MEMBER OF THAT AUGUST BODY! MARK? CAN YOU HEAR ME, BOY?

..AND PLEASE TRY NOT TO CALL ME "DEAR HEART" ON THE AIR, OKAY?

I WON'T, LUVY.

..AND THE PEOPLE OF VIETNAM ASSERT THEIR COMMITMENT TO A STRATEGY TO **END** THE ARMS RACE, AND TO DIVERT TO SOCIAL NEEDS THE UNTOLD BILLIONS THUS SAVED!

MR. PHRED, DOES VIETNAM HAVE SUCH A PLAN FOR OUR CONSIDERATION?

NOT YET, MR. SECRETARY. BUT WE HAVE SOMETHING JUST AS IMPORTANT— A DREAM!

WHAT SORT OF DREAM?

WELL, PRIMARILY, IT'S A DREAM OF A WORLD FREE OF FEAR, OF A TIME WHEN THE FAMILY OF MAN CAN TRULY WALK IN PEACE. OKAY?

DO YOU HAVE ANY LITERATURE?

UH.. NO, SIR. I THOUGHT IT WAS ALREADY IN THE CHARTER.